VERMONT

A Seasonal Celebration

VERMONT

A Seasonal Celebration

Photographs by Paul O. Boisvert

THE NEW ENGLAND PRESS, INC.
SHELBURNE, VERMONT

Printed in China by Regent Publishing Services, Ltd.

For additional copies or for a catalog of our other New England titles, please write:

The New England Press
P.O. Box 575
Shelburne, VT 05482

or e-mail *nep@together.net*

Visit our website at *www.nepress.com*

Boisvert, Paul.
    Vermont : a seasonal celebration / photographs by Paul O.
Boisvert. — 1st ed.
        p.   cm.
    ISBN 1-881535-30-4
    1. Vermont—Pictorial works. 2. Seasons—Vermont—Pictorial
works. I. Title.
F50.B65 1998
779'.99743—dc21
                                                            98-28735
                                                            CIP

CONTENTS

INTRODUCTION

$\mathcal{V}$ermont. On the map it looks insignificant, but its name looms large throughout the United States. What has come to be called the "Vermont mystique" is an image based on many factors, including fiercely defended natural beauty, an unhurried lifestyle, and an old-fashioned respect for craftsmanship and quality. The image is accurate. Vermont's landscape, seasons, and way of life contribute to a character that is identifiable and that sets it apart from all other places. A visit to any part of the state proves that this is not "Anywhere, U.S.A." It is unique. It is Vermont.

Vermont's stunning scenery is the subject of countless thousands of striking photographs, but Paul O. Boisvert's photography captures both Vermont's beauty and its special character better than that of anyone else. He grew up here, and the state is his lifelong subject. Boisvert's desire to find the best light, the best views, and the most dramatic scenes take him far and wide, and his knowledge of the state allows him to depict the essence of Vermont life. His razor-sharp vision focuses upon the striking rural scenes for which Vermont is famous, but his landscape is also populated by people enjoying their surroundings. His favorite subjects—sugarmaking, sailing, skiing—show the ways in which the Vermont countryside is used to best effect and why we so zealously protect it.

The title *Vermont: A Seasonal Celebration* accurately reflects what the photographs offer. The 131 images capture every season in many different contexts from all around Vermont. Sweeping panoramic vistas, scenic aerials, intimate portraits, and engaging images of people at work and play add up to a celebration of a wonderful state and a wonderful way to live.

Winter

Winter in Vermont is the way winter should be—long, cold, and, most years, white. For skiing, ice fishing, and snowmobiling to snowshoeing, snowboarding, ice sailing, and much more, Vermont's lakes and mountains offer a beautiful winter playground. The frigid, dry air yields views that are as breathtaking as the cold, and the customary blanket of snow softens the stark, frozen land.

Frozen landscape, Fairfax

DRAFT HORSES, WILDFLOWER FARM, LYNDON

Winter pasture, Jericho

HUNTINGTON

WORCESTER

ROCHESTER

7

JAYNES BRIDGE, WATERVILLE

SLEIGH RIDE, WAITSFIELD

Winter sun, St. Albans

Twenty-five below zero, Craftsbury

SNOWED IN, MARSHFIELD

DOG SLED, BROOKFIELD

WINTER FUN

In Vermont, the proverb says, there are nine months of winter and three months of poor sledding. It is no surprise, then, that Vermonters built the first ski lift in North America, popularized Nordic skiing, and fueled the snowboarding boom. Just about every Vermonter learns early how to have fun in cold weather—who knows what new winter thrills they will find next?

SKATING WITH FRIENDS, SOUTH HERO

CASEY'S HILL, UNDERHILL

SLEDDING OUTFIT, STARKSBORO

CROSS-COUNTRY, CRAFTSBURY

Up with the sun, Jay Peak

LOGGING, CABOT

CLEARING THE SNOW, LINCOLN

ICE CUTTING FESTIVAL, BROOKFIELD

CROSS-COUNTRY SKIING, INN AT THE ROUND BARN FARM, WAITSFIELD

*"In its whiteness, winter offers the human spirit a vast variety of pleasure and excitement. I
look forward to the ski trails on sunny days, and to the Northeaster blasting past the
windows on a stormy day."*

JOHN HOOPER, HOOPER'S PASTURE

AFTER THE STORM, FAIRFIELD

QUICK STOP, MONTGOMERY

WINTER MOUNTAINS

At one time, most people equated Vermont recreation with downhill skiing. Period. Now the mountains beckon visitors during all four seasons, and skiers share the slopes with boarders, telemarkers, and others. Ski areas remain a vital part of life in Vermont, though, and no matter how one gets down the mountain, a day on the slopes provides unmatched thrills and scenic splendor.

JAY PEAK

FALL LINE, STOWE

BOARDING, STOWE

SUGARBUSH

OKEMO

MOUNT MANSFIELD

Ice fishing, Lake Champlain

REFUGE, WATERVILLE

EAST CORINTH

Snowy night

PLEASANT VALLEY

BATTLING THE ELEMENTS, JERICHO

QUENESKA ISLAND, LAKE CHAMPLAIN

WELCOME SUNRISE, JAY PEAK

"It won't be warm until the snow gets off the mountain, and the snow won't get off the mountain till it gets warm."

From Talk Less and Say More

by WOLFGANG MIEDER

CAMELS HUMP

NIGHTLIFE, STOWE

MOONLIGHT, MOUNT MANSFIELD SUMMIT

Spring

JUST WHEN IT SEEMS THE LEAVES WILL NEVER OPEN, usually
sometime in mid-May, there comes a string of beautiful
spring days. The sunshine and warmth bring forth a
veritable burst of foliage and flowers. The yellow-green of
spring lasts only a short time before it deepens into the
rich green of summer, but for Vermonters, it is one of the
most eagerly awaited sights of the year.

SPRING GREEN, STARKSBORO

THE CHALLENGE OF MUD SEASON, ADAMANT

TOWN MEETING, STRAFFORD

WOODBURY

BAKERSFIELD

TOWN MEETING

March truly comes in like a lion most years in Vermont. With all the snowing and melting, mud and ice, cabin fever can start to set in, so what better time is there to gather with neighbors and iron out the town's business for the year? Town meetings last a long time and usually have lively debate, to be diplomatic, but they represent one of the last remnants of the grassroots democracy upon which this country was built.

WARREN

TAPPING THE TREES, FAIRFIELD

POURING SAP, DERBY

SUGARING

The mud season weather that frays nerves and roadways also yields Vermont's best-loved treats—maple syrup and maple sugar. Cool, sunny days and frosty nights get the sap flowing, and sugarhouses dotting the hills boil night and day to take advantage of the precious harvest. Vermont maple syrup over pancakes, ice cream, snow—almost anything, really—makes the wait for summer a lot sweeter.

BOILING, FAIRFIELD

DRAWING OFF THE SYRUP, LINCOLN

THE SWEET REWARD, PEACHAM

Working through the night, Fairfield

FANCY, GRADE B, AND EVERYTHING IN BETWEEN

New foliage, Cabot

STATEHOUSE, MONTPELIER

UNIVERSITY OF VERMONT, BURLINGTON

Apple orchards in bloom, Shoreham

Signs of spring, Stockbridge

MANCHESTER

BREAKING GROUND, BAKERSFIELD

SPRING PASTURE, CHARLOTTE

Summer

MORE AND MORE VISITORS are discovering what residents have always known—that summer is a terrific time to be in Vermont. Of course, in early summer it feels good just to put the winter coat in the closet for a while. Then it gets nice and warm—usually not too hot—and there is always more to see and do. Sunlight lingers long into the evening hours, but somehow the days quickly slip away.

SUMMER GLOW, HINESBURG

SUNRISE, CAMELS HUMP

WESTON

ECHO LAKE, CHARLESTON

ECHO LAKE, TYSON

60

Swimmers

Eye-level with the lake,
Skimmers of deeps opaque
See green steeps take
Ascent from the water line,
And in long sweeps combine
Bright birch and dusky pine.

JAMES HAYFORD,
Star in the Shed Window

Fun in the hot air, Quechee

CONNECTICUT RIVER, WATERFORD

NORMAN ROCKWELL BRIDGE, WEST ARLINGTON

A LONG AND WINDING ROAD, WESTMORE

Equestrian, Bennington

EARLY HARVEST, MONKTON

SUMMER RECREATION

Vermonters seize their precious time in the summer sun with a fervor built in the chill of November and March. After all, there are rivers and lakes perfect for fishing, splashing, paddling, and sunbathing. There are mountains to climb and trails to explore. There are yards and gardens to plant, mow, and dig. And when the work or play is done, there are shady spots to enjoy with a cold drink and a sigh of contentment.

BURKE MOUNTAIN

CLYDE RIVER, NEWPORT

KILLINGTON

FERRISBURGH

OTTAUQUECHEE RIVER, WOODSTOCK

Summer shower, Plymouth

BORDER TOWN, RICHFORD

Fourth of July, Burlington

LAKE MEMPHREMAGOG

SHELBURNE FARMS

FULL BLOOM, STOWE

Shelburne Bay

Spirit of Ethan Allen

Windsurfing

LAKES

Vermont has its own version of a great lake, Lake Champlain. It is but one of the beautiful lakes that help make summer in Vermont so much fun. From Champlain in the west to Memphremagog in the Northeast Kingdom to Harriman Reservoir near Massachusetts, Vermont's lakes attract pleasure seekers of all kinds to enjoy the clear, cool water.

LAKE MOREY

BURLINGTON BOATHOUSE

79

MALLETTS BAY

FARMSCAPE, UNDERHILL

Milking time, Enosburg

Enosburg Falls Dairy Festival

ORLEANS COUNTY FIELD DAYS, BARTON

Late summer dew, Marshfield

WEST CHARLESTON

Fall

Fall in Vermont is a time of great beauty and cheer, a celebration of gorgeous weather and stunning vistas of riotous color. Everyone enjoys fresh apples, pumpkins, and other bounties of the harvest. There is a touch of winter in the frosty mornings, but the crisp, refreshing days that follow provide ideal conditions for outdoor activities. Even after the tree branches are bare, Indian Summer days offer a last breath of warmth and soften the wait for snow.

Fall chore, Bristol

FALL IS COMING, STARKSBORO

STRAFFORD MEETINGHOUSE

EAST TOPSHAM

"*Fall in Vermont is a clarion call to all five senses. If a Vermonter is temporarily exiled to another state, the mention of fall will evoke memories of the taste, smell, sound, light, and color. But being in the middle of it is an intense sensory experience. We never believe that it can be so dramatic and yet find that each annual performance merits new superlatives.*"

MARGUERITE HURREY WOLF,
Of Cabbages and Kings

NORTHFIELD

Camels Hump

SHADOW LAKE, GLOVER

East Corinth

ADDISON

CABOT

WELLS RIVER

ST. ALBANS

FOLIAGE

Each year travelers flock to see Vermont's famous foliage display. Everyone searches for peak color, the fleeting time when nearly every tree has turned. The same sugar maples that provided delicious syrup six months ago star again in this show, turning brilliant orange and red. In a good year, the color becomes so luminescent and dramatic that the trees look almost unreal—then the leaves turn brown, fall, and winter is on its way.

FROSTY MORNING, MONTGOMERY

GRIGGS POND

WATERBURY RESERVOIR

Lake Willoughby

THE CHAMPLAIN VALLEY, MOUNT PHILO

"There are lots of ways we try to forecast what the coming winter will be. If my chipmunks retire early, it's supposed to be an ominous sign. If the fish in Lake Champlain strike for deep water early, they're trying to get away from the cold to come. Early geese overhead and extra honey in the hive tell you to get out your long-handled underwear."

RONALD ROOD,
A Land Alive

SNOW GEESE, ADDISON

Milkweed

GLOVER

ORCHARD BOUNTY, SHOREHAM

HARVEST

Commercial growers and home gardeners alike grow an amazing variety of produce. During Vermont's fall harvest, though, two crops dominate the scene: apples and pumpkins. Fresh, tangy apples are eaten out of hand or turned into delicious cider, pies, sauce, and so on. Pumpkins demand a more difficult decision— should they become pies and muffins or should they be saved for Halloween jack-o-lanterns?

MORSE FARM, MONTPELIER

HARVEST MARKET,
WAITSFIELD

PUMPKINHEADS

BROWNINGTON

SNOW ON THE MOUNTAIN, STOWE

A TASTE OF WINTER, UNDERHILL

CHURCH SUPPER, PEACHAM

PREPARING FOR THE FESTIVITIES

LUDLOW

HOLIDAY SEASON

The six weeks or so between Thanksgiving and New Year's Day are dark, cold, and usually quite dreary in Vermont. The funny thing is that it does not seem to matter—light, warmth, and goodwill define the season. People, regardless of their faiths and cultures, gather to enjoy good company and celebrate, and the glow of the holiday lights spreads good cheer far and wide.

ROUND CHURCH, RICHMOND

Danville Holiday Ball

Woodstock

Bristol

Holiday Spirit, Church Street, Burlington

PHOTO NOTES

Winter

2-3. After a heavy overnight snowfall I rose before sunrise and headed out. This was the first picture of the day. Nikon F4, 24 mm lens, 1/8 at ƒ16 on tripod

4. It was snowing hard when I arrived at the Wildflower Farm in Burke to photograph for a *Vermont Life* story on sleigh riding. Nikon F4, 24 mm lens, 1/15 at ƒ5.6 with Nikon SB24 flash

5. I had set out to take advantage of a beautiful day and a fresh fall of snow when this shot jumped out at me as I passed through Jericho. Nikon N90S, 28-70 mm lens, 1/250 at ƒ8

6. The fresh blanket of snow on the ground and in the trees creates a beautiful backdrop for this everyday scene of a Vermont farmer shoveling snow. Nikon F4, 80-200 mm lens, 1/250 at ƒ4.5

6-7. I knew this view would be great after a snowfall, so I rushed to get there before sunrise after a storm went through. I set up my camera and waited for the sun to barely illuminate the lower pine trees. Fuji GX 617 Panorama, EBC Fujinon 180 mm lens, 1/8 at ƒ32 on tripod with cable release

7. I was traveling in the hills above Rochester in the late afternoon when I passed by this well-kept farm. Nikon F4, 80-200 mm lens, 1/250 at ƒ5.6

8. Just north of Waterville I came across this scenic late afternoon covered bridge shot. Mamiya RZ 6X7, 65 mm lens, 1/15 at ƒ16 on tripod with cable release

9. Every year there is a sleigh ride festival in Waitsfield. You can always count on some great pictures at this event. Nikon F5, 20-35 mm lens, 1/350 at ƒ8

10. This beautiful winter sunset scene caught my eye as I drove south on I-89 just past St. Albans. Nikon F3, 300 mm lens, 1/30 at ƒ5.6 on tripod

10-11. After cross-country skiing all day at the Craftsbury Nordic Center, I headed home. Before I left town, though, I saw this beautiful deep blue pattern in a snowfield. Fuji GX617 Panorama, EBC Fujinon 180 mm lens, 1/4 at ƒ16 on tripod with cable release

11. The snow had really piled up this winter, as can be seen in this shot taken in Marshfield. Nikon F4, 35 mm lens, 1/250 at ƒ8

12. I was at the Brookfield Ice Cutting Festival when I noticed people having fun getting sled dog rides. Nikon FM2, 85 mm lens, 1/250 at ƒ4

12. My friend Rob Swanson and I like to skate. Here, we were sunset skating just off South Hero on Lake Champlain. Nikon N90S, 28-70 mm lens, 1/250 at ƒ5.6

13. I have been to Casey Hill to take pictures several times, but this time the sun came out after a fresh snowfall, and I knew the conditions would be perfect. Nikon F4, 50 mm lens, 1/250 at ƒ6.7

13. Sledding hills are part of the landscape in a Vermont winter. I took this photo on a hill in Starksboro. Nikon F4, 35 mm lens, 1/15 at ƒ5.6 with Nikon SB24 flash

13. I was working on a *New York Times* travel story about Craftsbury Nordic Center when I caught this skier enjoying the countryside. Nikon N90S, 85 mm lens, 1/250 at ƒ8

14-15. Jay Peak Ski Area is great, because you can find just about any kind of recreation there. I took this photograph while my friend Rob Swanson and I snowshoed the summit at sunrise. Nikon N90S, 28-70 mm lens, 1/125 at ƒ4

16. Traveling through the back roads of Cabot I came across this logger doing his job the old-fashioned way. Nikon FM2, 50mm lens, 1/125 at ƒ4.5

17. Brushing or scraping off the windows of your vehicle is a daily chore in winter here. I caught this man preparing to head out one late afternoon in Lincoln. Nikon F4, 85 mm lens, 1/250 at ƒ4.5

18. I was at the Brookfield Ice Cutting Festival when I caught this decisive moment. Nikon F4, 35 mm lens, 1/250 at ƒ6.7

18-19. The trails at the Inn at the Round Barn's touring center in Waitsfield were in perfect condition when I stopped to take this shot of a skier going by. Fuji GX 617 Panorama, EBC Fujinon 180 mm lens, 1/30 at ƒ16 on tripod with cable release

20. Overnight snowstorms often provide great conditions for taking pictures. After this storm I got up before sunrise to catch the early light on the new snow. Nikon F3, 35 mm lens, 1/250 at $f4.5$

21. I enjoy taking pictures during snow storms, so when I drove through Montgomery one snowy evening, I could not pass by without stopping to take this photograph. Nikon F4, 85 mm lens, 1/15 at $f4$ on tripod

22. On our first run at Jay after a nice snowfall the night before, my friend Rob Swanson said he was going for some big air. Nikon N90S, 28-70 mm lens, 1/250 at $f8$

22. Rob Swanson and I climbed to the top of the Chin on Mount Mansfield after the area received a foot of new snow. We skied the open snow field all the way to the bottom. Nikon N90S, 28-70 mm lens, 1/350 at $f5.6$

23. Snowboarding is becoming more and more popular. Here a boarder finds some fresh powder on a perfect day on the slopes of Stowe. Nikon N90S, 28-70 mm lens, 1/400 at $f5.6$

23. My friend Dave Howard and I skied Sugarbush after an overnight two-foot dump of fresh champagne powder. This photo shows why skiing Vermont is the best. Nikon N90S, 28-70 mm lens, 1/350 at $f5.6$

23. The skies were cloudy all the way on the drive to Okemo, but the sun broke through just as I was about to board the lift. Nikon N90S, 28-70 mm lens, 1/200 at $f4.5$

24-25. Skiing conditions were perfect, with fresh snow and dramatic skies, when my friend Dave Howard and I skied Stowe. We climbed the Nose of Mount Mansfield to ski on the fresh powder. Nikon N90S, 28-70 mm lens, 1/350 at $f5.6$

26. People always ice fish off Thompsons Point in Charlotte, so when I saw this beautiful sunset I rushed out to take this picture. Nikon F4, 80-200 mm lens, 1/60 at $f4.5$ on tripod

27. South of Waterbury I noticed these half moon barn door designs. Mamiya RZ 6X7, 127 mm lens, 1/15 at $f22$ on tripod with cable release

28-29. After a fresh snowfall and clearing skies I decided to travel to East Corinth for this early morning photograph. Fuji GX 617 Panorama, EBC Fujinon 180 mm lens, 1/8 at $f22$ on tripod with cable release

30. It was snowing like crazy when I hiked above Starksboro for this dramatic winter scene. Mamiya RZ 6X7, 127 mm lens, 16 seconds at $f8$ on tripod with cable release

31. One of the nicest drives in Vermont is Pleasant Valley at sunset. I photographed this winter farm with Mount Mansfield in the background. Mamiya RZ 6X7, 65 mm lens, 1/15 at $f16$ on tripod with cable release

32. It had just snowed about a foot and I was looking for pictures when I caught this jogger battling the elements in Jericho. Nikon N90S, 80-200 mm lens, 1/250 at $f6.7$

33. Driving along the end of Shelburne Point I came across this dramatic sunset on Lake Champlain. Mamiya RZ 6X7, 127 mm lens, 1/15 at $f16$ on tripod with cable release

34-35. I had been skiing at Jay Peak for three days when I decided to get up early to catch the sunrise at the summit. This photo shows the view looking south toward Mount Mansfield. Fuji GX 617 Panorama, EBC Fujinon 180 mm lens, 1/60 at $f11$ on tripod with cable release

35. I took this picture of Camels Hump from Huntington after a heavy snowfall. Nikon F4, 80-200 mm lens, 1/60 at $f5.6$ on tripod

36. The conditions were perfect for this long exposure: overcast skies, fresh snow, ambient light, and lots of traffic in Stowe. Mamiya RZ 6X7, 127 mm lens, eight seconds at $f16$ on tripod with cable release

37. I was driving home on Pleasant Valley Road in Underhill when the full moon rose over Mount Mansfield. Nikon F4, 300 mm lens, 1/30 at $f4$ on tripod

Spring

38-39. The new green of early spring is easy to see on this beautiful morning in Starksboro. Nikon F4, 80-200 mm lens, 1/30 at $f16$ with polarizing filter on tripod with cable release

40. I was documenting the very muddy back roads of East Montpelier when I happened upon this woman walking because her car was stuck in the mud over the hill. Nikon F4, 80-200 mm lens, 1/500 at $f4$

41. When I went to the Strafford Town Meeting I ended up staying the whole day and took some wonderful photographs. Nikon F4, 15 mm lens, 1/15 at $f5.6$ on tripod

42. I had been driving from one town meeting to another taking pictures when I came upon the residents of Woodbury still hard at work. Nikon N90S, 28-70 mm lens, 1/30 at ƒ5.6 with Nikon SB-26 flash

43. I attended town meeting in Bakersfield and photographed this woman casting her vote the old-fashioned way. Nikon FM2, 50 mm lens, 1/125 at ƒ2.8

43. Warren voters get back to work after lunch as they begin to wrap up the long day. Nikon N90S, 20-35 mm lens, 1/60 at ƒ4 with Nikon SB-24 flash bounced off ceiling

44. I photographed Brian Howrigan and his crew tapping trees in Fairfield. Nikon N90S, 50 mm lens, 1/200 at ƒ5.6

44. Larry Letourneau of Derby Line has one of the most beautiful sugarbushes I've ever seen. Nikon F4, 35 mm lens, 1/125 at ƒ4.5

45. I was visiting the Robert Howrigan Sugarhouse in Fairfield when things started getting a little hot. Nikon F4, 24 mm lens, 1/8 at ƒ8 on tripod

45. I came across this old-time sugarmaker in Lincoln just as he was drawing off maple syrup. Nikon F4, 20-35 mm lens, 1/15 at ƒ4 with Nikon SB-24 flash bounced off ceiling

45. I was traveling through Peacham one late afternoon when I ran across this roadside bargain. Nikon F4, 50 mm lens, 1/125 at ƒ5.6

46-47. I was driving around Fairfield looking for sugarhouses with good ambient light when I found this perfect scene. During the time exposure I turned my car headlights on the sugarhouse for about five seconds. Nikon F4, 35 mm lens, five minutes at ƒ5.6 on tripod with cable release

48. I used Robert Howrigan's sugarhouse in Fairfield for this dramatic shot of window-lit maple syrup. Mamiya RZ 6X7, 127 mm lens, 1/8 at ƒ16 on tripod with cable release, white lighting 1,200-watt flash outside with remote trigger

49. I was driving the back roads of Cabot looking for maples in bloom when I stopped to take this photo. Nikon F4, 50 mm lens, 1/60 at ƒ5.6 with polarizing filter

50. I was passing the Vermont Statehouse when I noticed the contrast of the deep blue sky and golden dome. Mamiya RZ 6X7, 127 mm lens, 1/15 at ƒ22 on tripod with cable release and polarizing filter

51. It was late afternoon on a bright spring day when I drove by the UVM green and saw that all the trees were in bloom. Nikon N90S, 28-70 mm lens, 1/125 at ƒ8

52. This splash of white against green caught my eye as I drove through Stockbridge late in the day. Nikon F4, 80-200 mm lens, 1/250 at ƒ5.6

52-53. I was traveling south along Lake Champlain when I came upon this orchard of apple trees in full bloom. Fuji GX 617 Panorama, EBC Fujinon 180 mm lens, 1/15 at ƒ22 on tripod with cable release

53. The valleys of southern Vermont were exploding with fresh new foliage when I came across this photo in Manchester. Nikon FM2, 180 mm lens, 1/250 at ƒ4.5

54. The growing season is short in northern Vermont. I caught these farmers working to get their spring planting done north of Bakersfield. Nikon N90S, 80-200 mm lens, 1/250 at ƒ6.7

55. A herd of cows takes advantage of the new spring foliage at the base of Mount Philo. Nikon N90S, 28-70 mm lens, 1/200 at ƒ6.7

Summer

56-57. It had been an ugly day, dark and rainy, when the clouds started to break up late in the afternoon. Suddenly the sun came out, illuminating the underside of the dark clouds and producing this spectacular rainbow. Nikon F4, 24 mm lens, 1/15 at ƒ5.6 on tripod with cable release

58. I waited for the perfect conditions at the right time of year to get this photo of the sun rising over Camels Hump. Nikon F4, 300 mm lens, 1/60 at ƒ5.6 on tripod

59. Passing through Weston at sunset on a gloomy, rainy day, I was surprised to see the clouds break up. I scrambled through wet underbrush to reach this viewpoint and took a long exposure of the waterfall. Nikon F4, 50 mm lens, one second at ƒ16 on tripod with cable release

60. The light and the movement of the swimmer in Echo Lake combined to create a dramatic pattern in the water. Nikon F4, 80-200 mm lens, 1/250 at ƒ4.5

60-61. This nice panoramic of Echo Lake in Charleston captures the appeal of Vermont's many small lakes and ponds in summer. Fuji GX 617 Panorama, EBC Fujinon 180 mm lens, 1/30 at ƒ22 on tripod with cable release

62. I went to the Quechee Balloon Festival in Woodstock and was rewarded with a beautiful morning with no wind. Nikon F4, 80-200 mm lens, 1/250 at f4.5

63. It was a stunning, electric green day when I took this shot while flying over the Connecticut River and photographing the landscape. Nikon F4, 50 mm lens, 1/500 at f4

64. Having spent the night in southern Vermont I was able to get this sunrise photo of the famous covered bridge in West Arlington. Mamiya RZ 6X7, 127 mm lens, 1/8 at f22 on tripod with cable release

65. I was in the Northeast Kingdom photographing a travel story for the *New York Times* when I took this picture of bikers along Lake Willoughby. Nikon F5, 300 mm lens, 1/250 at f5.6 on tripod

66. I was photographing the Vermont Bicentennial Heritage Journey for *Vermont Life* magazine when I captured these silhouettes of three girls and their horses on a ridge top. Nikon F4, 80-200 mm lens, 1/250 at f4.5

67. The light on this hay barn caught my eye as I traveled through Monkton to Bristol. Nikon F5, 85 mm lens, 1/250 at f6.7

68. Anglers try their luck on the Clyde River in Newport as evening sets in. Nikon N90S, 80-200 mm lens, 1/200 at f4

68. This sunrise photo from the top of Burke Mountain shows some of the wilderness in the Northeast Kingdom. Nikon N90S, 20-35 mm lens, 1/125 at f8

69. Mountain biking is a popular summer recreation at ski areas. I took this shot at Killington while on assignment for the *New York Times*. Nikon F4, 35 mm lens, 1/250 at f5.6

69. Dick Raymond has his own golf course in Ferrisburgh. I used late afternoon light for a dramatic effect. Nikon F4, 50 mm lens, 1/250 at f6.7

69. On my way to Woodstock I stopped to get this shot of a fisherman on the Ottauquechee River. Nikon FM2, 105 mm lens, 1/250 at f4.5

70-71. A solitary canoeist braves the rain on Woodward Reservoir in Plymouth, just off Route 100. Nikon F4, 50 mm lens, 1/125 at f2.8

72. I caught this bridge scene while I was in Richford, near the Canadian border, taking pictures for *Vermont Life* magazine. Nikon F4, 85 mm lens, 1/250 at f4.5

73. This view of Burlington's Fourth of July celebration was taken from on top of the Radisson Hotel on the Lake Champlain waterfront. Nikon F4 with 35 mm lens, 1/2 at f8 on tripod with cable release

74-75. I was taking photographs of the Northeast Kingdom when I captured this image of Lake Memphremagog. Fuji GX 617 Panorama, EBC Fujinon 180 mm lens, 1/15 at f16 on tripod with polarizing filter and cable release

76. I was on assignment photographing Shelburne Farms for the *New York Times* travel section when I took this photo of the Inn at Shelburne Farms. Nikon F4, 300 mm lens, 1/125 at f8 on tripod

77. I was looking forward to lunch at Whiskers Restaurant in Stowe when I noticed the gorgeous flowers on the grounds. Nikon N90S, 20-35 lens, 1/200 at f8

78. I was on my own sailboat preparing to start a race when I saw this dramatic scene of a B class race off Red Rocks Park. Nikon FM2, 80-200 mm lens, 1/250 at f4

78. I was admiring this sunset over Lake Champlain when the Spirit of Ethan Allen came by to make this photograph really work. Nikon F4, 300 mm lens, 1/250 at f4.5

78. I was in my power boat looking for pictures when I came across this windsurfer on Lake Champlain. Nikon F4, 80-200 mm lens, 1/500 at f4.5

79. I had been circling Lake Morey looking for just the right late afternoon photo when I came across this passing sailboat. Nikon N90S, 85 mm lens, 1/250 at f6.7

79. I was in my power boat headed to Burlington for lunch when I noticed this huge storm cloud providing a backdrop for the Burlington Community Boathouse. Nikon F4, 35 mm lens, 1/125 at f4

80-81. I took this shot of the start of the Thursday night races in Malletts Bay from a small dinghy. There wasn't much wind for sailing, but the conditions were excellent for taking pictures. Nikon FM2, 24 mm lens, 1/250 at f6.7

82. Passing through Underhill at sunset I noticed the light on this classic barn. Nikon F4, 80-200 mm lens, 1/60 at f8 on tripod

83. I was on my way to Enosburg Falls on a perfect Vermont summer day when I came across this farmer herding his cows. Nikon F4, 80-200 mm lens, 1/250 at f6.7

84. I was shooting the Enosburg Falls Dairy Festival for *Vermont Life* magazine when I took this photo of spectators and contestants at the horse pulling contest. The photo ended up on the cover of the magazine, and the cover was selected the best regional magazine cover in the U.S. that year. Nikon F3, 300 mm lens, 1/125 at *f*5.6 on tripod

85. I captured this image of harness racing at the Orleans County Field Days in Barton. Nikon F4, 80-200 mm lens, 1/500 at *f*4.5

85. I was at the Orleans County Field Days when I photographed this light moment at the ox pulling contest. Nikon F4, 80-200 mm lens, 1/250 at *f*4

86. Late summer mornings start to get crisp and cool, with heavy dew. This spider web in the sun caught my eye at the start of a beautiful day. Nikon N90S, 50 mm lens, 1/100 at *f*3.5

87. I had just left Morgan and was on my way to Charleston when I caught the last of this dramatic sunset. Nikon FM2, 24 mm lens, 1/15 at *f*8 on tripod

Fall

88-89. Traveling through Bristol I caught this man mowing his lawn. Mamiya RZ 6X7, 127 mm lens, 1/30 at *f*16 on tripod with cable release

90. I was flying around the Champlain Valley with my brother Maurice in his 1938 Piper Cub when I caught this early fall photo of Starksboro. Nikon F4, 50 mm lens, 1/500 at *f*4

91. I set up my tripod in Strafford to capture this dramatic view of the church. As I was taking pictures these two people walked past me and into my photo. Nikon F4, 24 mm lens, 1/30 at *f*11 on tripod with polarizing filter

92-93. I was in East Topsham looking for the perfect panoramic when I came across this view. Fuji GX 617 Panorama, EBC Fujinon 180 mm lens, 1/8 at *f*22 on tripod with polarizing filter and cable release

93. This gazebo and the brilliant foliage behind it in Northfield made a nice fall subject. Nikon N90S, 50 mm lens, 1/15 at *f*16 on tripod with polarizing filter

94. During an unusually brilliant fall season I decided to take advantage of a clear day and fly around Camels Hump to take pictures of the foliage. Nikon F4, 28-70 mm lens, 1/500 at *f*4.5

95. A calm day turned Shadow Lake in Glover into a good mirror for reflecting the hillside above it. Nikon N90S, 20-35 mm lens, 1/200 at *f*6.7

96-97. I had been walking around the town of East Corinth when I spotted this great panoramic. Fuji GX 617 Panorama, EBC Fujinon 180 mm lens, 1/15 at *f*22 on tripod with polarizing filter and cable release

97. The sun had just risen on a cold, clear morning when I came across this photograph in Addison. Nikon N90S, 80-200 mm lens, 1/200 at *f*4

98. On the back roads of Cabot I came across this tunnel of fall color. Mamiya RZ 6X7, 127 mm lens, 1/15 at *f*22 on tripod with cable release

99. Just west of Wells River I caught this brilliant maple in full color. Mamiya RZ 6X7, 65 mm lens, 1/15 at *f*22 on tripod with cable release

99. I photographed this couple biking through the foliage in Taylor Park in St. Albans while working on a story for *Vermont Life* magazine about people using the bike train to Vermont. Nikon F4, 20-35 mm lens, 1/250 at *f*6.7

99. These maple leaves show us what's ahead on a very cold fall morning. Nikon F4, 50 mm lens, 1/125 at *f*4

100-101. On my way to Irasburg the brilliant reds above Griggs Pond caught my eye. Fuji GX 617 Panorama, EBC Fujinon 180 mm lens, 1/8 at *f*22 on tripod with polarizing filter and cable release

102. During another great foliage season I went flying with my friend Howard Fisher. We flew directly to Waterbury Reservoir, where I took this photograph. Nikon F4, 50 mm lens, 1/500 at *f*4

103. It was a beautiful crisp fall day when I took this late afternoon photo on Lake Willoughby. Nikon N90S, 80-200 mm lens, 1/250 at *f*5.6

104-105. On a crisp fall morning I ventured out in search of photographs and ended up on top of Mount Philo in Charlotte. Fuji GX 617 Panorama, EBC Fujinon 180 mm lens, 1/30 at *f*16 on tripod with cable release

105. I was flying with my brother Maurice when this dramatic view of snow geese over the Dead Creek Wildlife Area caught my eye. Nikon F4, 85 mm lens, 1/500 at *f*4

106. On a frosty fall morning just down the road from my house I photographed this milkweed pod. Mamiya RZ 6X7, 127 mm lens, 1/30 at *f*11 on tripod with cable release

107. I came upon this scene in Glover while traveling through the Northeast Kingdom. Nikon N90S, 28-70 mm lens, 1/250 at *f*8

108. Shoreham is full of apple orchards. I caught this farmer about to move a small fraction of his bounty. Nikon F4, 35 mm lens, 1/125 at *f*4

108. The sun came out from behind thick clouds just as I was passing Morse Farm in East Montpelier to produce this very colorful photograph. Nikon N90S, 50 mm lens, 1/200 at *f*6.7

109. These farmstand pumpkins are catching the early morning light in Waitsfield. Nikon N90S, 20-35 mm lens, 1/15 at *f*16 on tripod

109. I was buying some apples at a Shoreham roadside stand when I noticed these artistic jack-o'-lanterns. Nikon F4, 85 mm lens, 1/125 at *f*5.6

110-111. It had been a brilliant fall. In this photo I captured a late afternoon scene in Brownington. Mamiya RZ 6X7, 127 mm lens, 1/4 at *f*32 on tripod with cable release and polarizing filter

112. Hearing that the mountains had gotten an early season snowfall the night before, I knew that this location would provide a great sunrise photo. Nikon F5, 80-200 mm lens, 1/60 at *f*8 on tripod with cable release

113. It had snowed for most of this late fall day. I was passing through Underhill when the sun broke out just before it set. I climbed on the roof of my truck and took this photo. Nikon F4, 35 mm lens, 1/15 at *f*4 on tripod

114. I love church suppers and the people they bring out. I queried a few magazines about a photo essay about them, but none went for it. I decided to assign myself to the job and ended up selling lots of photos

from it. Nikon F4, 20-35 mm lens, 1/15 at *f*4 with Nikon SB-24 flash bounced off ceiling

115. My friend Dave Howard and his children Chris and Megan return from a successful trip to find the family Christmas tree in Bakersfield. Nikon F4, 85 mm lens, 1/250 at *f*5.6

116. This image captures the glow of a Vermont Christmas in Ludlow. Nikon F4, 20-35 mm lens, 1/4 at *f*8 on tripod with cable release

116. A cloudy dusk with snow on the ground created perfect conditions for capturing the glow of the interior lights of the round church in Richmond. Nikon F4, 20-35 mm lens, 1/8 at *f*8 on tripod with cable release

117. I documented the Danville Holiday Ball for *Vermont Life* magazine. I didn't want the flash coming from the camera so I mounted a white lighting 1,200-watt unit with a softbox off to the side. I remote fired the flash for this effect. Nikon F4, 24 mm lens, 1/15 at *f*5.6

117. Christmas lights illuminate this striking covered bridge in Woodstock. Nikon F4, 35 mm lens, 6 seconds at *f*16 on tripod with cable release

117. I was searching for Vermont Christmas scenes using ambient light when I came across this firehouse in Bristol. Nikon F4, 50 mm lens, 1/8 at *f*8 on tripod with cable release

118-119. I had been waiting for this exact combination—fresh snow, Christmas lights, and perfect ambient light—for quite some time. I parked my car on Bank Street, climbed onto the roof with my camera and tripod, and took this photo. Nikon F5, 50 mm lens, 1/4 at *f*5.6 on tripod